D0516041

Measure It!

How Do You Measure
Time?

by Thomas K. and
Heather Adamson

CAPSTONE PRESS
a capstone imprint

Yippee!

Vacation is coming in one month.
Ann's family is going on a ski trip.

How long will one month take?

A month is longer than a week.
But it's shorter than a year.

People around the world measure time the same way. Short bits of time are measured in seconds, minutes, and hours.

Longer amounts of time are measured in days, weeks, months, and years. Ann has many things that measure time in her house.

Clocks measure seconds, minutes, and hours. The fast-moving pointer moves every second. It takes 60 seconds to go around the clock. Sixty seconds equals one minute. The minute pointer takes one minute to move to the next mark. The hour pointer takes 60 minutes to move to the next number.

Watches are small clocks.
Ann's dad looks at his watch.
He tells Ann it's time for school.

Calendars keep track of longer amounts of time. Each month gets a page.

JANUARY

Sunday	Monday	Tuesday	Wednesday	Thursday	Friday	Saturday
					1	2
3	4	5	6	7	8	9
10	11	12	13	14	15	16
17	18	19	20	21	22	23
24 31	25	26	27	28	29	30

FEBRUARY

Sunday	Monday	Tuesday	Wednesday	Thursday	Friday	Saturday
	1	2	3	4	5	6
7	8	9	10	11	12	13
14 My Birthday	15	16	17	18	19	20
21	22	23	24	25	26	27
28						

Ski Week

MAY

Sunday	Monday	Tuesday	Wednesday	Thursday	Friday	Saturday
						1
2	3	4	5	6	7	8 Dance Recital
9	10	11	12	13	14	15
16	17	18	19	20	21	22
23 30	24 31	25	26	27	28	29

JUNE

Sunday	Monday	Tuesday	Wednesday	Thursday	Friday	Saturday
		1	2	3	4	5
6	7	8	9	10	11	12
13	14	15	16	17	18	19
20	21	22	23	24	25	26
27	28	29	30			

SEPTEMBER

Sunday	Monday	Tuesday	Wednesday	Thursday	Friday	Saturday
			1	2	3	4
5	6	7	8	9	10	11
12	13	14	15	16	17	18
19	20	21	22	23	24	25
26	27 Mom's Birthday	28	29	30		

OCTOBER

Sunday	Monday	Tuesday	Wednesday	Thursday	Friday	Saturday
					1	2
3	4	5	6	7	8	9
10	11	12	13	14	15	16
17	18	19	20	21	22	23
24 31	25	26	27	28	29	30

MARCH

Sunday	Monday	Tuesday	Wednesday	Thursday	Friday	Saturday
	1	2 First Soccer Practice	3	4	5	6
	8	9	10	11	12	13
	15	16	17	18	19	20
	22	23	24	25	26	27
	29 Spring Break	30	31			

APRIL

Sunday	Monday	Tuesday	Wednesday	Thursday	Friday	Saturday
				1	2	3
4	5	6	7	8	9	10
11	12	13	14	15	16	17
18	19	20	21	22	23	24
25	26	27	28	29	30	

JULY

Sunday	Monday	Tuesday	Wednesday	Thursday	Friday	Saturday
				1	2	3
	5	6	7	8	9 Dad's Birthday	10
11	12	13	14	15	16	17
18	19	20	21	22	23	24
25	26	27	28	29	30	31

AUGUST

Sunday	Monday	Tuesday	Wednesday	Thursday	Friday	Saturday
1	2	3	4	5	6	7
		Camping Week				
8	9	10	11	12	13	14
15	16	17	18	19	20	21
22	23	24	25	26	27	28
29	30	31 First Day of School				

NOVEMBER

Sunday	Monday	Tuesday	Wednesday	Thursday	Friday	Saturday
	1	2	3	4	5	6
7	8	9	10	11	12	13
14	15	16	17	18	19	20
21	22	23	24	25	26	27
28	29	30				

DECEMBER

Sunday	Monday	Tuesday	Wednesday	Thursday	Friday	Saturday
			1	2	3	4
5	6	7	8	9	10	11
12	13	14	15	16	17	18
19	20	21	22	23	24	25
26	27 Winter Break	28	29	30	31	

A calendar shows how many days and weeks are in a month. Ann's big ski trip is next month.

It's hard to wait for vacation to come. Ann tests what each amount of time feels like.

How many times can Ann jump rope in one minute? Ann jumps 50 times.

10

A minute feels like a short time when she's jumping rope. But it feels long when she tries to hold her breath.

An hour is longer than a minute.

Ann's ballet class lasts one hour. All that spinning and jumping is a good workout!

She's glad to rest and watch a movie. A movie lasts about two hours.

A whole day lasts from midnight to midnight.

A day has 24 hours. Most days, Ann gets up and goes to school. Later, she spends the evening with her family. But today is Saturday. Ann is sleeping in.

Sunday	Monday	Tuesday	Wednesday	Thursday	Friday	Saturday
21 No School	22	23	24	25	26	27 No School
	├—	— School	Days —	—	—┤	

16

Seven days equals one week. Some things happen once a week. Ann has Spanish class at school each Monday. Family game night is every Friday. Hurry before time runs out!

A month is about four weeks long. Ann and her family go to the library once a month. Ann will find books to read before vacation.

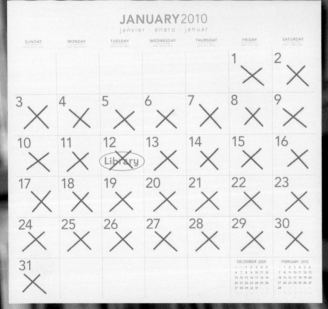

Ann's birthday comes once a year.
A year is 12 months long. Last year
Ann was 7 years old. Now she is 8.
Next year, Ann will be 9 years old.

FEBRUARY2010
février · febrero · februar

SUNDAY	MONDAY	TUESDAY	WEDNESDAY	THURSDAY	FRIDAY	SATURDAY
	1 ✕	2 ✕	3 ✕	4 ✕	5 ✕	6 ✕
7 ✕	8 ✕	9 ✕	10 ✕	11 ✕	12 ✕	13 ✕
14 My 8th Birthday	15	16	17	18	19	20
21	22	23	24	25	26	27
28						

├── Ski Week ──────────┤

FEBRUARY2011
février · febrero · februar

SUNDAY	MONDAY	TUESDAY	WEDNESDAY	THURSDAY	FRIDAY	SATURDAY
		1	2	3	4	5
6	7	8	9	10	11	12
13	14 My 9th Birthday	15	16	17	18	19
20	21	22	23	24	25	26
27	28					

It doesn't take as long as a birthday for vacation to come. It has been a month. Ann finishes her library books.

Ann's family leaves tomorrow!

Vacation time is finally here!
Ann packs her suitcase. Vacation
will last one week.

**That's seven days
of fun!**

Ann's Ski Vacation

There are so many ways to measure time—the seconds they smile for pictures, the minutes they laugh, and the hours they ski.

Only a few vacation days are left. Then Ann will have to wait a whole year until ski trip time comes again.

Cool Measuring Facts

• Before clocks, people used sundials to tell the time. The sun would shine on the sundial. The shadow the dial created pointed to what time it was.

• It takes 29.5 days to go from one full moon to the next full moon.

• A cheetah can go 100 feet (30 meters) in one second at its top speed.

- Stephen Clarke carved a face into a pumpkin in 24 seconds. That time is a world record.

- How long does it take you to eat a slice of pizza? Josh Anderson ate a whole pizza in one minute, 45 seconds.

- Kiev, Ukraine, has the world's largest floral clock. The clock face is 54 feet (16.5 meters) across and is made of flowers.

Glossary

calendar—a chart showing all the days, weeks, and months in a year

clock—a tool that tells time; the hands on a clock point to the hour, minute, and second

day—a 24-hour period, from midnight to midnight

hour—a unit of time that is equal to 60 minutes

measure—to find out the amount of something

minute—a unit of time that is equal to 60 seconds

month—one of the 12 parts that make up a year

second—a very short unit of time

week—a period of seven days

year—a period of 12 months

Read More

Dowdy, Penny. *Time.* My Path to Math. New York: Crabtree, 2009.

Hutchins, Hazel. *A Second Is a Hiccup: A Child's Book of Time.* New York: Arthur A. Levine Books, 2007.

Scheunemann, Pam. *Time to Learn about Seconds, Minutes, and Hours.* Time. Edina, Minn.: Abdo, 2008.

Internet Sites

FactHound offers a safe, fun way to find Internet sites related to this book. All of the sites on FactHound have been researched by our staff.

Here's all you do:

Visit *www.facthound.com*

Type in this code: 9781429644594

Index

A+ Books are published by Capstone Press,
151 Good Counsel Drive, P.O. Box 669, Mankato, Minnesota 56002.
www.capstonepub.com

Printed in the United States of America in North Mankato, Minnesota.
112010
006003R

Books published by Capstone Press are manufactured with paper
containing at least 10 percent post-consumer waste.

Library of Congress Cataloging-in-Publication Data
Adamson, Thomas K., 1970–
How do you measure time? / by Thomas K. and Heather Adamson.
p. cm.—(A+ books. Measure it!)
Summary: "Simple text and color photographs describe the units
and tools used to measure time"—Provided by publisher.
Includes bibliographical references and index.
ISBN 978-1-4296-4459-4 (library binding)
ISBN 978-1-4296-6332-8 (paperback)
1. Time—Juvenile literature. 2. Calendar—Juvenile literature. 3.
Units of measurement—Juvenile literature. I. Adamson, Heather,
1974– II. Title. III. Series.
QB209.5.A335 2011
529—dc22   2010002787

Credits
Jennifer Besel, editor; Juliette Peters, designer; Sarah Schuette,
photo studio specialist; Marcy Morin, studio scheduler; Laura
Manthe, production specialist

Photo Credits
All photos by Capstone Studio: Karon Dubke except: Shutterstock:
Alegria, 26 (blue skis, white gloves), Aleksandra Nadeina, 26
(mountain), ravl, 28 (moon), VeryBigAlex, 26 (winter scene), Vladimir
Wrangel, 26 (cabin)

Note to Parents, Teachers, and Librarians
The Measure It! series uses color photographs and a
nonfiction format to introduce readers to measuring concepts.
How Do You Measure Time? is designed to be read aloud to a pre-
reader, or to be read independently by an early reader. Images
and narrative promote mathematical thinking by showing that
objects and time have measurable properties, that comparisons
such as longer or shorter can be made between multiple objects
and time-spans, and that there are standard and non-standard
units for measuring. The book encourages further learning by
including the following sections: Cool Facts, Glossary, Read More,
Internet Sites, and Index. Early readers may need assistance using
these features.